Aviothic Warcloud

AN AMALGAMATION OF EMOTIONS

ATHIKA SHAN

Contents

1. Sun Up 7

2. An Eternal Emotion 11

3. Pure and Perfect 15

4. Beyond Doubt 17

5. Lost Meanings 19

6. Magic-A 21

7. Magic-B 23

8. Spin and Roll 25

9. A View in the Dark 27

10. Breathe 29

11. Ebullience 31

12. Balance 33

13. Chaotic and Calm 35

14. Vow 37

15. Bluebell 39

16. With Glee 41

17. To Yourself 43

18. Miss You 45

Contents

19. Desires..47

20. Jealousy..49

21. Free From Pride.....................................51

22. I & I...53

23. Alive..55

24. Memories..57

25. Life is Laurel..59

26. Perpetuate...61

27. Ahead of All...63

28. Alas...65

29. Aviothic..67

30. Away..69

31. Moira (One's Fate or Destiny)....................71

32. Fika (A Moment to Slow Down and
     Cherish Things).....................................73

33. Forbearance...75

34. Celestial Sphere....................................77

35. Morosis...79

36. Pink and Blue.......................................81

37. Verse Scribbler......................................83

38. Lambent Lady.......................................85

39. The Mirror Not an Error...........................87

40. Elysian...89

41. Sciamachy (A Battle Against Your Own Imagination) 91

42. Little Lines 95

43. Conquering 97

44. Boil a Bit 99

45. Hourly Hopes 101

46. Attached 103

47. Finding the Pleasant 105

48. Smiles for Miles 107

49. Pocession So Special 109

50. In My Hands 111

51. Shielded 113

52. Born in the Wrong Era 115

53. Moments 119

54. Right and Not Fright 121

55. Just You 123

Beyond Grateful 125

Aviothic Warcloud

1

Sun Up

Tea cups and coffee mugs
Waking us up in the mornings
And making up the day...
Salt and sugar sprinkled
To make my meal sparkle
Breeze made with
Ingredients of air and movement
That make me stand calm
What's better than the best
If I'm blessed?
The sun in the west and we can rest
The moon as the guest
Soon is when I tune
Coated in white
Pure as a soul
Can I paint yourself
With the colours of my dream?
The air is filled with me
And I can't say how
The screen goes down,

Moon moves around
Gritty for some more
Newspaper and milk
Maybe a teacup or a coffee mug
I don't know wat I desire for
But really deserve to be me!

2

An Eternal Emotion

A soul that knows that
I'm not perfect
And still stares at me
Maybe my mess meant a lot
Do I seem never bothered?
Yet explaining you to the moon...
Still having me stuck inside myself
Mighty enough to pretend
Catching a cloud
Or finding a cliff
Yet searching comfort
A simple hello
Heals all havocs
A path paved with
Platinum dust
Soil seeded with gold
Leaves of emerald
And blossoms of birthstones...
Roses and rubies are remixed
For no reason,

Undisturbed by the sun, sounds and souls
Let's just spend now
Time tied tight
Sonars sound silly
For our depth
And we have comforted death
For no dare
But divine enough...
A path paved with
Platinum dust
Soil seeded with gold
Leaves of emerald
And blossoms of birthstones...
Roses and rubies are remixed
For no reason,
Undisturbed by the sun, sounds and souls
Let's just spend now
Time tied tight
Sonars sound silly
For our depth
And we have comforted death
For no dare
But divine enough...

3

Pure and Perfect

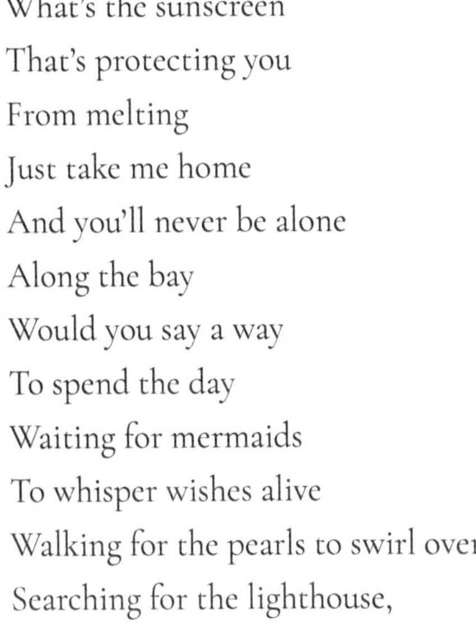

What's the sunscreen
That's protecting you
From melting
Just take me home
And you'll never be alone
Along the bay
Would you say a way
To spend the day
Waiting for mermaids
To whisper wishes alive
Walking for the pearls to swirl over
Searching for the lighthouse,
That finds my destination.

Aviothic Warcloud

4

Beyond Doubt

Like a snowball
Something rolls in...
Yet something sat in my mind
Trying to find
Don't preserve or prevent your power
Prove the power
Creating everything with your heart
Can never fake anything...

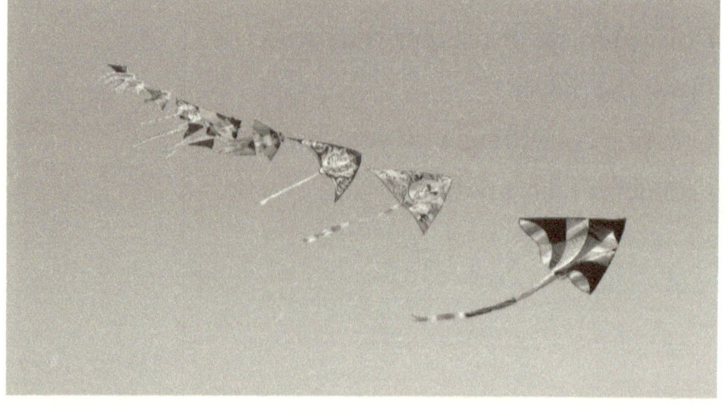

5

Lost Meanings

Why won't all my endemic burdens
Fly away like a free kite?
No one hears my words
I just can't understand the theory behind
Potencies are to be priced
It's time to rewrite
And invite light
Don't turn right or left
But hug yourself tight
Feel lite as a kite...

6

Magic is public
You just have to mind it!

Aviothic Warcloud

7

Magic-B

Fairy tales have no ages

No matter if you are

Deep in the dark

Or blessed in the bright

Magic is everywhere

And don't forget to mind it

We have lashes the loves magic

Ears that evolve around music...

As rare as perfect eyebrows

You are......

Indeed, your fairy tale is fair enough

Nothing requests you to loose hope

And something would find You the great

That serves you with pleasure and peace...

As rare as perfect eyebrows you are!!!

Aviothic Warcloud

8

Spin and Roll

Let's spin a wheel
Pass a card, toss a coin
Or roll a die
The one is for a reason,
A two that rescues,
Maybe a three can free me
Or a four that makes me roar
And a five that arrives...
A tail or a head???
For this fairy's tale,
that you can just mail...
a six that tricks all... so,
find a seven if its heaven!
Eight and you are not late,
Nine and you are pristine
There rolls a ten
For this, young women
A tail or a head
There are lots ahead
And I am a young lady
Ready to twirl!!!

9

A View in the Dark

It's so hard to thank yourself
And take myself back
Smiles are endless responses
Sometimes to greet and to keep going
But this time, it is to say goodbye and keep moving
There is a lie found in light
That no one bothers
Let's add some extra frosting to our cakes
When hate has hostility
Love carries courage...

Aviothic Warcloud

10

Breathe

Your ethics would be your north star
Making you sartorial,
To make your novel good enough
With chapters of pride and shame...

Aviothic Warcloud

11

Ebullience

Be the roots

Be the steam

Grow your leaves

Be the flowers

Bear the fruits

At times don't forget

To be your rain

And always be your sunshine!

Aviothic Warcloud

12

Balance

Life with a bossy brain
And a heavy heart is laden.

13

Chaotic and Calm

Don't search a stage,

when the world is your stage...

strive for the stay and

sum up your speed,

Wishes are being whispered

Between are blessings

Being blown...

Eternal energies that

evolve as emotions

many malice and more myths

solving all the stealthies seen

age not a cage

but just a message

carrying courage with no shortage

A voyage to stage at any age...

When you could philosophise your moments......

Aviothic Warcloud

14

Vow

What's the fuel that drives me insane
What for is the robbery in reality?
Where is all the long dark wavy curls?
Maybe lost along with
the rose gardens...
and it's not all done yet
still in the lion's den
waiting to win...

Aviothic Warcloud

15

Bluebell

Knowing is the kingdom
Of knowledge
While kindness is its king!

16

With Glee

When the clock climbs midnight
And I'm sure for a scoop
of ice cream on my cone...
when I could watch
the hour hand glide graciously
while I flit above an empty flyover...
And yet...
The darkness is not over
Let me find a twirl
For the pearls and curls of mine
To stay slick...

Aviothic Warcloud

17

To Yourself

What's locked in my eyes?

Why is my mind frozen?

Something took its role as gravity

It simply pulls everything down!

Live like light

Don't escape yourself

But be elusive...

18

Miss You

If I can't hear the city noise

Nor can I inhale the country's calmness,

If I can't let the waves

Wash all my shells away,

If I cannot find

The sun set until I rise,

If I cannot hide the horizon

Hung between,

If I cannot feel my fineness ahead,

Without you!

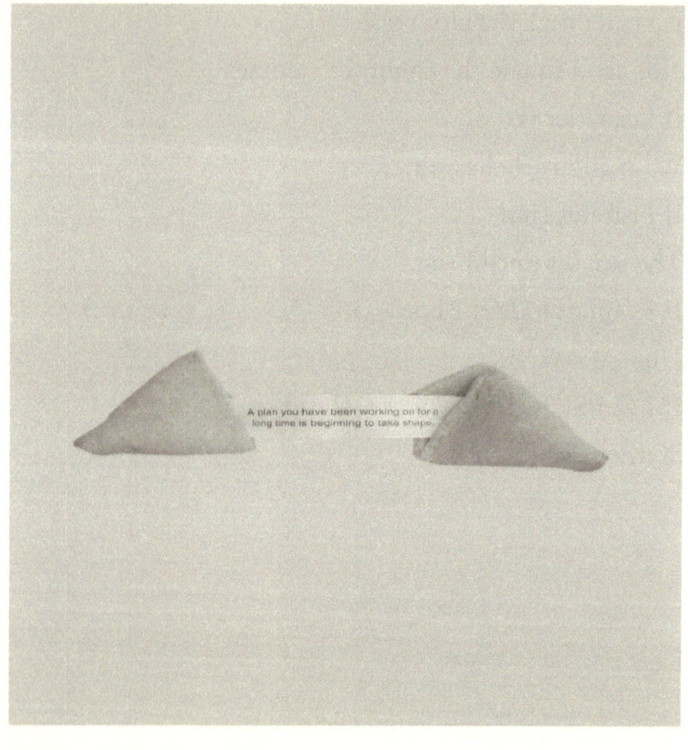

Aviothic Warcloud

19

Desires

With, unspoken desires
Luck was not unleashed
While deigning a destiny,
Finding fellowship
And fortune...
Still waiting with
Unspoken desires...
It's not a secret with intense meaning...
But, still a desire
Kept inside as fire
And meant not to be said...
Not an empty heart...

20

Jealousy...

Make the sun jealous
With your morning blink
Let every new hour
Of yours, feel jealous
Of the already hour
Speak words, that
Challenge with your
Words on paper...

Aviothic Warcloud

21

Free From Pride

Dear humans of the twenty first century,
Throw away the two edged sward your catching hold of...
Which either blames yourself or others.
Maybe it's a bidding war
Binding all of us...
Be aware of their austerity
And awaken your humility.

Aviothic Warcloud

22

Eternal nightmares

Insane daydreams

While the sky is busy pouring

And sometimes soulful with its shine

Some mapping new paths

And some dancing to the tunes...

It's always me, filling colours

In illusions and imaginations...

Aviothic Warcloud

23

Alive

Waiting for new changes,
Illusions settled in a latibule
Wishing for the other phase of life...
Altering myself along
Wanting to taste more seasons!!
Mornings that are late
Where nothing seems exciting
Attending classes online
When nothing seems breathing...
Letters that meant nothing
Who should I find
If everyone else seems busy
Will I have a space to fill
Vast is all
Witnessing a tune to say
Enough to escape...

24

Memories

Never felt like rewriting
A few past moments...

Aviothic Warcloud

25

Life is Laurel

Life is laurel with well cut diamonds

In everyone's face

Life is beautiful

With its own ups and downs

Just like a waterfall

From fins to wings

In between stands our limbs!!!

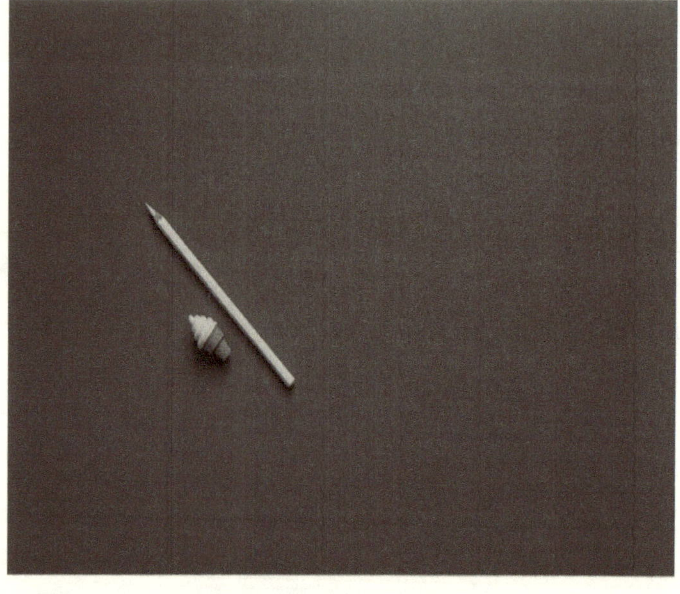

Aviothic Warcloud

26

Perpetuate

Felt like the white pencil

Or the divider found in every geometry box...

Don't try to find my stimulus

Cause I can't spare time on a hide and seek...

Engaged In delight

With fair amount of pain...

Trying to put myself on the line of life,

playing the strings of faith.

Some are penned to be framed

But I was penned by blame...

Still promised like gravity

To never go back!

27

Ahead of All

Hire some honesty
Until you write your own spell...
Own your humility
Until heaven's door unlocks...
Enchant your ethics everyday
Until it evolves the earth...

28

Alas

Everyone's asleep
Maybe deep in dreams
And here I am
Trying to create!
All I do is accidentally tear pages...
Missing friends
And feeling lost
Rewinding the past
Allowing myself to regret a bit
Thinking its not fair to leave
myself incomplete...
with infinite thoughts
and it's not ok to lack identity
while it's hard to create one!

29

Aviothic

Barefoot on the grass

And everything seems to be true

I have a jar besides me

With a lady butterfly

While I feel so decreased...

The days are so lifeless

When goals of golds

Were just jokes

Barefoot on the grass

And I have myself unleashed!

My blood caught its vein

Together with the heart on its beat

And everything seems so true......

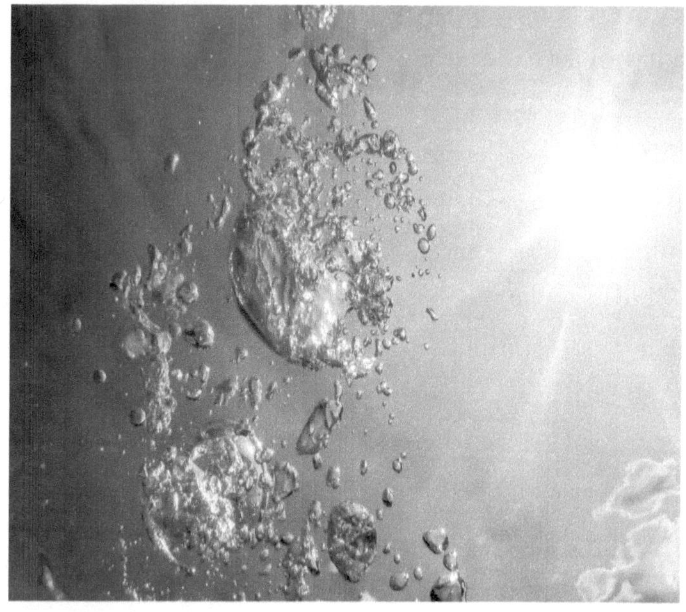

30

Away

Fly yourself out of guilt,
And glide in glory of life!
Fly yourself out of stress,
And see in all surprises!
Fly yourself out of cry,
And take wing for a new sky!
Swim into a fresh beam,
And paddle away all your loss!
As you leave a sinking ship
Throw all your heavy hearts,
And swim over the tides!
Not easy to be tired,
And not hard to try...

Aviothic Warcloud

31

Moira (One's Fate or Destiny)

I cannot see my path clearly

I rub my eyes

And seem to lose my lashes

Dwelling in faith

A day or more to feel or heal the pain...

Aviothic Warcloud

32

Fika (A Moment to Slow Down and Cherish Things)

Just like nuts in my chocolate
That's spread all over my bread
You make it a lot clumsy and crispy
Now, make a promise to keep on
Upgrading your flavour!

33

Forbearance

I still have a long way to go
Until everything falls
In focus and I give it a click!
There are many pages written
Some, soaked in tears
And some are even painted!
I believe in my desires
Still, there are a lot more pages
To bear masterpieces!

Aviothic Warcloud

34

Celestial Sphere

You have your own sky,
With faith fixed in it.
Open to shower on you,
Exhibit rainbows,
Scatter light of gold and silver,
Stars up there which seem to love you...
Maybe your north star is stuck up there!
Sagacity surviving inside of you
Moving in the world of yours
Capturing all what you need
With desires being vigilant and wild...

Aviothic Warcloud

35

Morosis

Engrossed in emotions

Crying inside my heart

Wanting you to hear all them

The pain is endemic

Myself meant "morosis"...

Aspirations seemed to fail,

Which made me fly, float and fade away...

36

Pink and Blue

This is not the time for stories,

A pleasant minute

Not to write future stories

And not for reading out stories of the past.

Not the pair,

But why not? At least

an eye gets its sleep?

All deeds with no greed!

INK

37

Verse Scribbler

Until it pulls myself
Deep in and let in
Destroy the inner peace
With respect to all wreckage
Expecting no worries,
A mind that triggers minds
Just waits to find
Its heart surprised
And you are blessed!

38

Lambent Lady

Oh, you lambent lady!
Witness every battle
With no fear,
Your mind is a magical mixture
Desire for your
Dignity with a deed,
Oh, you lambent lady!
No great deal for your leal
Just don't promise yourself
Prove your power!
Perhaps, you are not my lot my love lost
You are just my lasting love...
Oh, you lambent lady,
Your, adore has authority
And no destiny!
A sapphire in fire...
As like an entire flare...
Oh, you lambent lady!

39

The Mirror Not an Error

A meter in front
All of a unique font,
Not for a say
And it's the way
The sunshine of your sky
And you can fly,
Remember to own you
And not to zone you!
Admire the fire inside
And take a minute of
Your courage to look more
A rose garden in fire
Maybe for the glory of a glose
And you are so close
Plus, not to lose.
Your scars not heard
Maybe scary,
Every star is beautiful by its fall,
Just a tall wall,
Now, raise your lashes
And just ask for yourself...

Aviothic Warcloud

40

Elysian

Paper and pen the best pair
To make pride the rifest,
Peculiar enough to transform everything
With no self doubt...
Just an arrangement
Of 26 letters,
And rearrangement for better!
Forever in my palms,
Running across pages
And no cages to restrict...

Aviothic Warcloud

41

Sciamachy (A Battle Against Your Own Imagination)

It's not fair here
As a fairy tale is...
Tis not my dark hair this time,
That's free in the dark night...
Tis not about throwing if
You are not gonna catch it
Between the gentle giants
And tiny terribles are us
Let's correct this a bit...
It is not really fair
And, actually not perfect...
This place is not perfect
But a powerful palace...
Don't let words out
Your lips and tears out on fear...
Your cry is often not heard
But all roars are royal enough!

Bees buzz, lions roar,
Flamingos balance, flowers blossom
And cannot be denied
You and me are great
But, never have shared a treat...
No one refuses to grow up
But still to show up...
Standing still and resting
my hands on my chin,
my stand begins to
lean on a nearby,
experiencing the pleasure
for a new start with hope...
and it's not a hoax
the power of promises never let go,
Not a final feeling
Of finding the year's fun...
HAPPY NEW YEAR!!!

42

Little Lines

My biggest mistakes were
My biggest crimes
Doors always shut, but
Floors never forget to open another
A dreamy ladder that always
Invites me for an uplift...
Which in, has my target...
It makes me never regret
Which paints my wounds
With colours and bounds me divine...
So, it's all fine to go blind for a day
But not today,
Because you have surprises to see...

Aviothic Warcloud

43

Conquering

Hey, look at me!
I know the value
Of something but
Not everything!
A year is not a fear anymore
Cause I've already failed!
An hour is all power now,
As I've been powerless
Problems with any rhythm,
Is no more a handsome hoax...

44

Boil a Bit

Watch the waves coil by

And don't boil your self

Winter hints trees and

Leaves bow down

Spring rings the land

While the butterflies kiss your cheeks...

Now watch the waves and trees

But don't freeze!!!

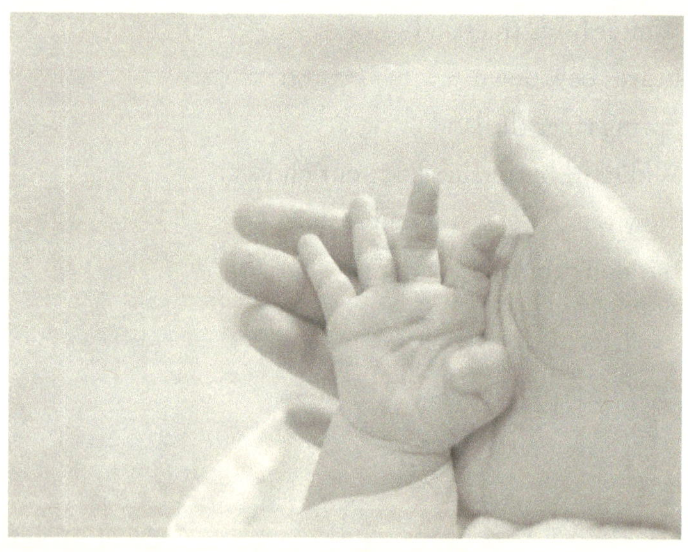

45

Hourly Hopes

Maybe not today
But another day,
Just sway for a play
Is not all for the way,
Seconds and hours
With minutes in between,
Days and months
With weeks in between,
All the way across
Every moment for
Brains and hearts with hope in between!

Aviothic Warcloud

46

Attached

As a feather on the floor

Surrounded with souls

that believe...

The sky cannot be tied

But rolls a wave wide

A path of gold dust

That never invites anyone...

A jar of happiness, locked

And the keys lost...

Limitless thoughts that always fought...

If yes, your eyeballs glow,

As magical was the magnetic movement

And I found myself always in its field

Never counted the stars as it

Was only you who shined!!!

Looking into the mirror for months

As the mirror borrows

A window to witness all my ways wise...

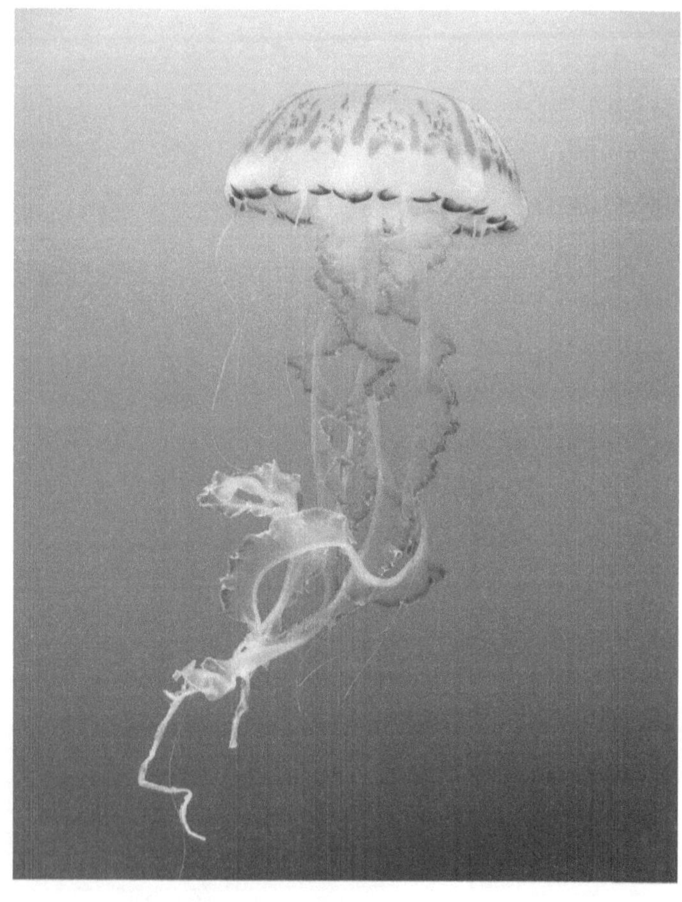

47

Finding the Pleasant...

Make a heart smile
At the worsts,
And every cry by joy
Every moment is made eternal...
I was not made in heaven
Nor am I worth it?
But its all heaven
In and around
And I am just so fond...

Aviothic Warcloud

48

Smiles for Miles

Smiles that are wide
And dimples that are deep
All with a heap
To hide rooted.
Silver or gold, may it shine
as better, like wine
And let smiles, be wide...
As the silver highlights
With enough stories
To be filled in pages
And an unfaded smile
That has been pure
For miles of years......

Aviothic Warcloud

49

Pocession So Special

A relationship, where friction is false
Everything is stuck to the
Edge of your memory...
Everyone else lacks the empathy
While you embrace it...
Then time was not owned
Nor was it registered to something else...
But just waiting for you
To fill in the moments
And now feeling the thread so, thin
But not so tight...
Without moving air
Here I am so quietly aching
Unenviable umbrella
That I am catching hold of...
Awaiting, for sunbeams
And a colourband...
Now heavy hearted
But never half hearted.

50

In My Hands

Whose orphaned poem
Is lying on the table,
that no one bothers to label.
I'm not a story teller to
take a lot of time...
I can squeeze the lime
With fine flavours...
As smooth as a feather, landing
That the soil bears
Lovely as a lavender breeze,
May this moment freeze...

51

Shielded

I haven't seen volcanoes explode,
I have felt them inside myself
Well, its not a happy Hawaii
Vacation in there...
All my paper boats seem to sink
And paper rockets fall off...
Illness occupied inside
It's a Wissen
Like a farmer trying to save
His crops from fire
Here I am breathing
In the void of perseverance
And hope tucked within...

52

Born in the Wrong Era

Love for A line dresses
Secretly wishing to wear
Mini skirts and Go-go boots,
Understanding chronologies
And wishing, to find my days
In the past era,
Making my makeup pop out
My eyes to drag the focus
Long letters that travelled miles
To reach hands...
Pleasure of poems that Sounded
like your loved souls everyday...
tunes of typewriters to "The Twist",
holding my hands tight
to feel my heart beat
trying to find the wind
that carries me back to the era,
Infront of my infinite eyes,
Indulged in every line of this poem,

An era that existed early,

Is, all is what I wished for...

Stuck and swaying in the 60s is myself,

Now, I agree to set myself free

In this era's story!

Aviothic Warcloud

53

Moments

Moments when I wanted
Time to pass by quickly
So that, I could reach
The moment I wanted to be in...
I still enjoyed the absence
of a time machine that did not exist...
The wait felt as if, my whole
Life was behind my closed lashes
Filled with pleasure...
Moments when I wanted
Time to stay still...
So that, I could be saved
From embarrassing, awkward
And the not so desired scenes in life...
It was not supposed to be a big issue
But was always big in its own value......

54

Right and Not Fright

Its all right to be weak
If you are not a wreastler,
Its all right to be a fool
If you don't rule,
Maybe a wrong number picked by a plumber
Can fix my puzzle meant!
Its all right to be steady and speedy
If it's a highway
And nothing is fright if God is on board!

55

Just You

If it's a choice, don't reside,

If it's a choice don't let me decide!

Thoughts that, echoes in your mind

And ya, sure

It's as messy as a Saturday night!

Oh! Stars that twinkle all night long,

The sun that shines, your mornings bright

With some layered lightings

White space that was ventured with ink

And was precious to be left unerased!

What so ever has enabled

All the time you've been in

Filled with opinions and options

It was just you to decide your destiny...

Now, find your ticket to your moon!

Beyond Grateful...

I took this page to offer my earnest thanks to all the wonderful people out there, who perpetuated me.

The very first thanks goes to my parents who made me lucky enough for all the opportunities and the much needed feedbacks.

Thanks a ton, mom... For giving a wider view of the world and for percolating integrity in myself.

To my grandparents, for emboldening me.

With a full heart, I humbly thank Mr. Mohan uncle, for all his kind words of advice and continuous support.

And am really pleased to have my initial guidance from Ms. Parvathy aunty during my childhood in the United Kingdom.

I express my sincere appreciation to my educators for all their guidance and motivation.

Last but not least, my dearest friends and my brother for being my first reader.

With love + respect,
Athika Shan